Victoria Findlay Wolfe

15

MINUTES OF PLAY

Improvisational Quilts

Made-Fabric Piecing • Traditional Blocks • Scrap Challenges

C&T PUBLISHING

Text and Photography copyright © 2012 by Victoria Findlay Wolfe

Photography and Artwork copyright © 2012 by C&T Publishing, Inc.

Publisher: Amy Marson

Creative Director: Gailen Runge

Art Director: Kristy Zacharias

Editor: Liz Aneloski

Technical Editors: Ann Haley and Teresa Stroin

Cover/Book Designer: April Mostek

Production Coordinator: Zinnia Heinzmann

Production Editor: Alice Mace Nakanishi

Illustrator: Zinnia Heinzmann

Quilt Photography by Christina Carty-Francis and Diane Pedersen of C&T Publishing, Inc., unless otherwise noted; How-To Photography by Monica Buck, unless otherwise noted

Published by C&T Publishing, Inc., P.O. Box 1456, Lafayette, CA 94549

Library of Congress Cataloging-in-Publication Data

Wolfe, Victoria Findlay, 1970-

15 minutes of play--improvisational quilts : made-fabric piecing - traditional blocks - scrap challenges / Victoria Findlay Wolfe.

pages cm

ISBN 978-1-60705-586-0 (soft cover)

1. Patchwork--Patterns. 2. Quilting--Patterns. 3. Improvisation in art. I. Title. II. Title: Fifteen minutes of play--improvisational quilts.

TT835.W642 2012

746.46--dc23

2012015424

Printed in China

10 9 8 7 6 5 4

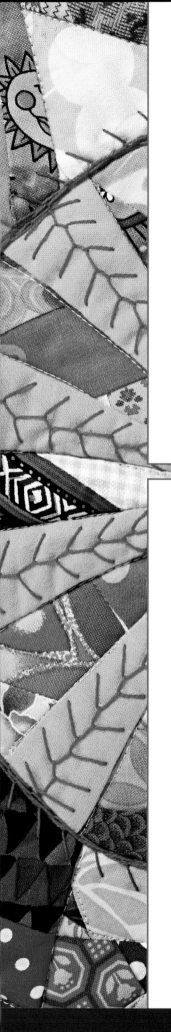

Dedication

For my loving husband, Michael, and beautiful daughter, Beatrice, who put up with my scraps trailing behind them when they walk across the room, who lovingly laugh at me when they pick threads from my sweaters, and who encourage me to keep doing what makes me happy—making quilts.

This book is in memory of my grandmother Elda Wolfe. I have only realized in the last couple years just how much this strong woman influenced everything I do as an artist. My happiest childhood memories were at her house. At the age of seven, I decided that I would one day be a happy old person sitting in my rocking chair with a big old smile on my face looking back at my life, knowing I lived my life in a way that brought me pure joy. The last time I saw my grandmother, she said to me, "Well, I hope you're happy." And indeed I am.

Acknowledgments

Thank you to all my quilter friends who have encouraged me, commented on my blogs, and joined me in play, for at least 15 minutes, along the way. A big thank-you to:

Bonnie Cummings Bus, for her pure, honest thoughts each week.

Jackie Kunkel, for her steady faith and support of my many projects.

My mother, for her help—to see her rekindle her love of sewing through my projects has been amazing.

Tonya Ricucci—if I had not found your blog, I may not have gone down this road of obsessive quiltmaking! You pointed me to quilters I had never heard of, such as Gwen Marston, Roberta Horton, and Anna Williams.

A big thank-you to **The Rebels in Seattle**, for taking me into their nest and making me feel a part of a community of like-minded quilters.

Finding people who love to make quilts and share my joy in creating makes each and every day great. Happy quilting!

Contents

My Inspiration 6

What Is Play? Why Play? Why 15 Minutes? 14

Four Easy Techniques for "Made-Fabric" 28

Free-Pieced Made-Fabric 30

Paper-Pieced Made-Fabric 36

Five-Sided Made-Fabric 40

The Weekend Scrapper Experiment 42

Fast-and-Easy Made-Fabric 44

16 Quilt Blocks to Get You Inspired 48

1 Half-Square Triangle 49

2 Sawtooth Star 49

3 Mod Strips 50

4 Giant Whirlygig 51

5 X Marks the Spot 52

6 Lady Fingers 52

7 Scrapped Shoo Fly 53

8 Split Square 53

9 Square in a Square, Squared 54

10 Elda's Flower 54

11 Scrap Star 55

12 Sawtooth Square 55

13 LeMoyne Star 56

14 Flying Geese 58

15 Slashing 58

16 Twister 59

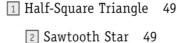

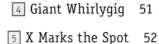

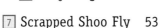

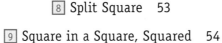

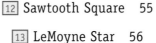

11 Challenges to Get You Going 63

Challenge #1:

Make a quilt entirely from clothing.   63

Challenge #2:

Force yourself to use every last bit of fabric
your scrap partner sends you.   66

Challenge #3:

Mix solids and prints.   68

Challenge #4:

Focus on warm and cool colors.   71

Challenge #5:

Use fussy cutting.   73

Challenge #6:

Use fabric you don't think you can use.   76

Challenge #7:

Make the quilt you said you'd never make.   78

Challenge #8:

Mix up your new blocks with your old blocks and find a way
to bring the past to the present.   81

Challenge #9:

Let movement be the key to your quilt.   85

Challenge #10:

Make a medallion quilt from a set of previously made blocks
that never grew into a quilt.   87

Challenge #11:

Build a quilt purely on intuition.   89

In Closing 93

About the Author 95

My Inspiration

Victoria's Double-knit Crazy Quilt, Elda Wolfe, 1988, 74″ × 85″

I grew up on a farm in Minnesota with scrap quilts on my bed—a lot of them. The more the merrier—and warmer! Our house was only heated with wood stoves, and in the morning when the stoves had burned out, it was cold. We'd grab our school clothes and slip them on while staying under the layers of quilts. I'd lie awake at night, tracing the patterns of color as one blended into another on my grandmother's crazy quilts. Little did I know that they would inspire me for the rest of my life.

My father had an upholstery business on the farm, and one of the first things I learned to sew were pillows, by hand, using upholstery fabrics from his outdated sample books. He kept his scrap batting for future projects, so I wasn't allowed to stuff my pillows with it. Instead, I had to find an alternative—tissues. As you can imagine, these pillows were not only hard, but scratchy too. The coolest thing I remember learning was to use a blind stitch to close up my pillows. They looked seamless without any topstitching; to me, they looked professional.

My mother was a great seamstress. She often made our clothes and also enjoyed adding decorated 6″ lengths to the bottom edge of my pants, so they wouldn't be "high waters." Usually, when a family member was getting married, my mother would get out her Singer and make some quilt tops. Then the quilt frame would come out—my brother and I had the job of knotting the yarn ties.

Sewing was always around me. My mother has many stories of my creativity around the sewing machine. She loves to tell about the time she was sewing when I was a toddler; annoyed that she wasn't giving me attention, I snuck off and ate her lipstick.

When I was older, I had a glue sewing machine to make Barbie clothes. But mostly, I learned to sew things by hand with whatever scraps I had around. I guess some things don't change; my life revolves around my scraps to this day!

In junior high school, I became the sewing wiz, creating stuffed dogs, duffle bags, and hand-sewn patchwork pillows. In high school, I made shirts, 1980s-style jumpsuits, and a long pink wool coat with a gray silk lining. Recovering from a broken leg at age 15, I kept myself busy attempting to hand appliqué a quilt block with three little chicks under an umbrella. It was torture! (The appliqué, not the broken leg.) It wasn't until three years ago that I started appliquéing again.

My Inspiration: Elda Wolfe—Quilter, 1918–2005

Donna Mae's Crazy Quilt, Elda Wolfe, 1990, 70″ × 81″

Victoria and Elda Wolfe, 1987

My grandmother Elda Wolfe was an arthritic invalid by the age of 45. Because of this, her fingers and elbows did not bend well. So, she would perch herself in her rocking chair by the living room window and watch life go on around her.

Grandma Elda loved puzzles. This is evident in her quilts. She often sat in that rocking chair with a dime-store card table set up in front of her with either a puzzle or a quilt on it. When she worked on a quilt, she would keep a bag of double-knit scraps strewn out on the table in front of her and a sheet in her lap. She would carefully pick each piece, place it in position, look at it, and quickly decide whether it was the right one. Then, she would sew it down with big, red embroidery floss X's. She would work a few pieces at a time, letting the quilt emerge. Rarely did she cut a piece of fabric to fit a particular space. She had a real knack for creating depth that is bold and exciting. Her use of lights and darks—and everything in between—presents a stunning array of movement and fluidity that many of us find difficult to achieve.

The back of my grandmother's quilt top is as exciting as the front! Looking at the rainbow of colors of thread and the stitches she used has taught me a lot about her process.

Why did she use double-knit fabrics? In the mid-1970s, my mother worked for two years sewing clothing and winter coats for Fingerhut, a mail order catalog. She would buy 6-foot-long bags of scraps for 50 cents to take to my grandmother. Grandmother's arthritis in her hands made it difficult for her to work with some fabrics. She enjoyed the double knits because they did not fray, therefore she did not have to turn the edges under.

As a child, I could often be found sitting at the kitchen table with a huge bag of those scraps. With an ink pen and a 3″ × 3″ cardboard template, I would trace squares all over the fabrics, leaving room to cut them out with a ¼″ seam allowance. It was always an eyeball sort of process, and that is how I first learned to do patchwork.

Double-Knit Red, White, and Blue, Elda Wolfe, 1983, 74″ × 79″

I traced and cut out the squares in this quilt at my grand-mother's kitchen table.

Marianne's Crazy Quilt, Elda Wolfe, 1977, 73″ × 83″

My grandmother's love of using what she had, using scraps, and doing jigsaw puzzles gave her great satisfaction. I know that feeling. She passed on to me that same passion for creating beautiful things from what I have—whether it's gardening, canning, saving old clothes, or making quilts. Her process meshes with mine—today we use everything we have because it makes sense, rather than out of necessity. I also like a good, hard puzzle. (Grin!)

Flower pillow, Elda Wolfe, 1983, 15″ × 15″

Flowers in Elda's Garden, Victoria Findlay Wolfe, quilted by Shannon Baker, 2010, 46″ × 64″

After looking at the way my grandmother put fabrics together, I went about making a version of her technique that reflects the way I approach making fabric for my quilts. I like parts of a quilt to surprise you—a block that was intentionally made wonky or a new color added in. This quilt gives me such joy, as I can see just how much my grandmother has influenced the way I approach fabrics.

Realizing that my grandmother is the inspiration behind nearly everything I create—knowing where I came from, who I am now, and where I am going—gives me a sense of peace. If she were here today to see the quilts I make, she would have a good old chuckle.

Judy's Crazy Quilt, Elda Wolfe, 1981, 67″ × 80″

My Journey

I always knew I would be an artist. I went to college to be a fine artist and studied painting, photography, and graphic design. For the first twenty years after college, I focused on fine arts. However, the opportunity to sew a shirt or a quilt for a friend kept appearing in my life.

Girdle Bones in Primary (1 of 2) 1997 (painting) and *Intuition Quilt* 2010 (on the bed), both by Victoria Findlay Wolfe (Full image of *Intuition Quilt* is on page 89.)

Mister's Baby Quilt, Victoria Findlay Wolfe, 2002, approximately 30″ × 24″

Mister's Baby Quilt was one of my first quilt commissions. When I was asked to make this quilt, I had only made two or three quilts and was more of a seamstress than a quilter. I brought out one of my grandmother's hand-sewn quilts for inspiration, because it was the only homemade quilt I had in my home. Looking at it, I knew two things:

1. I loved all the colors running this way and that. Memories flooded back as I examined the quilt, just as I had done as a child. I knew I had to include that scrappy feature.

2. I knew hand sewing would take too long, so I needed to find a way to make a quilt like that, but by machine my way. I also knew the client wanted something unique and original, so I thought this style of quilt would do the trick.

I had no idea how to bind a quilt, so I just used the pillow-turn method I had learned from watching my father make cushions in his upholstery business. To me, sewing was play. I approached it the same way that I approached painting a canvas—starting from the inside and working outward, using up whatever I had, and looking at color and angles. I enjoyed playing with the fabrics so much that I became obsessed with making more and more quilts.

When I was a new mother, I had very little time to myself, so I would set aside 15 minutes a day for my creative time. As an artist, when I sit down to draw, I do 10-second sketches and 30-second sketches. As a photographer, I take 60–70 images, only keeping a few.

When I started to make sewing my full-time creative path, I needed a way to get my creative energy flowing. I had a lot of ideas, but where should I begin? So, sticking with what I knew, I would warm up by making little collages from my fabric scraps, put them aside, and play a bit more. This way, I could watch as patterns I liked and color schemes I thought were interesting happened completely by accident.

Eventually, I realized I could take those little blocks of "Made-Fabric" and make something useful from them. They fulfilled my need to create something in a short amount of time.

One day in 2008, while searching for canning recipes online, I did an Internet search for "homemade." By accident, I found Tonya Ricucci's blog. Many of you know her as Lazy Gal or the Unruly Quilter. I saw her beautiful quilts, which are made in a process I had never heard of—improvisational-style quilting. That moment changed everything for me. It gave me permission to keep doing what I was doing, while also giving me a community of peers from whom I could find support and inspiration. It confirmed that I had found my creative journey.

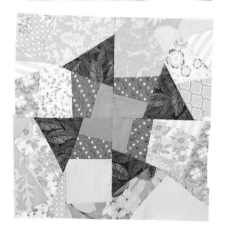

What Is Play?
Why Play?
Why 15 Minutes?

What Is Play?

Play is different for everyone. Even though we are adults, we all still have that childlike sense of what play is. Whether you are a new or a seasoned quilter, there is always room for play—to reconnect to the curiosity you had as a child.

For me, play through improvisational piecing helps me find a path to move forward with a project. I enjoy every part of the discovery process. In fact, love of the *process*, rather than of just the finished object, is what keeps me sewing and quilting.

Why Play?

Play plants seeds of creativity and encourages you to find a different way to approach your quilts. Trying something different that is out of your usual routine can be scary, but it will spark your creative inspiration.

Play through quilting brings together ideas and creativity—relationships of color, texture, and fabrics. It also keeps the ideas coming. It helps you use what you already know about quilting and forces you to try new things. Play encourages a new direction and keeps your creative process open to all the wonderful possibilities. As you sew a few pieces together—like putting pieces of a puzzle together—your mind is gathering information. As each "bit" is added to the bigger picture, things become clearer, which helps you move forward.

While playing, you'll have *aha!* (happy accident) moments along the way. One patch of fabrics can send you off on a new idea, colorway, or design.

Play + Inspiration = Creativity

Why 15 Minutes?

As a creative person, I have found that I *must* create every day. Sometimes it is difficult to find the time to sit and sew every day, but if I make it a habit to carve out 15 minutes each day for creative exploration through play, I have accomplished my goal.

Play is nonlinear thinking. Playing with my scraps takes me to my creative process fast and helps me improvise quickly as challenges present themselves. I often find that my 15 minutes turn into a half hour or even all day, giving me a freedom I might not have found otherwise. I work in a traditional / improvisational style. I find that the more I play to work out my designs, the more clearly my path becomes.

Working quickly in small blocks of time makes me loosen up, and ideas start swirling in my head and last much longer than the 15 minutes I sat piecing new Made-Fabric. (I use the term "Made-Fabric" to describe my improvisationally pieced fabric.) During those 15 minutes, I am forced to stop thinking about the outcome and to focus on completing the piecing: grab, place, and sew. I decide later how the blocks will be used.

What Play Looks Like to Me

I sew just to make new Made-Fabric.

I look at what I am making and notice things.

I ask questions:

Do I see anything I like?

What colors or patterns am I drawn to?

I make choices—I don't fret too long over decisions, I just go with it!

I follow my intuition!

I make more Made-Fabric!

After making some pieces of Made-Fabric, I realized in one of my play sessions that I loved all the polka dots peeking out at me. I did not set out to make fabric for a polka dot quilt, but I made the fabrics and allowed the discovery to happen. Once I decided I liked the polka dots, I dug out all the dots I had in my stash and cut 2″, 3″, and 4″ strips of each piece. I sliced them up into random bits and added them to my scrap bin. As I grabbed fabric scraps, I incorporated those dots into all my Made-Fabric. I knew I would decide later what would become of the blocks I was creating. One step at a time—at this moment, I just focused on making the blocks. *Polka Dots Squared* (page 43) is the result of this play.

Polka-dot Made-Fabric blocks on a design wall

Dot Calm, Karen Griska, 2011, 24″ × 24″

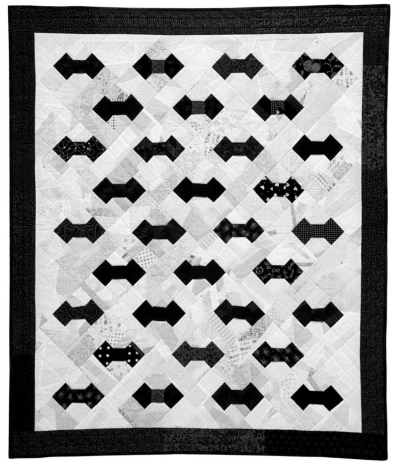

Black Tie Affair, pieced and quilted by Helen Beall. Blocks contributed by 15 Minutes Play Quilt Bee Players: LeeAnn Decker, Beth Shibley, Glenda Parks, Sujata Shaw, Margaret Cibulsky, Shelly Pagliai, Charlotte Pountney, Mary Ramsey Keasler, Helen Beall, Brenda Suderman, Lynn O'Brien, and Victoria Findlay Wolfe, 2011, 50″ × 58″

One Journey through the Creative Process

Here is an example of play leading to inspiration: I was going to a sewing retreat, but I could not decide what project to bring along. Mostly, I wanted to have fun and chat with my peers, so I wanted something that did not require my full, serious attention. I started with my usual warm-up of randomly sewing scraps from my big scrap bin to make fabric.   Strategy

While I pieced, I noticed that my fabric choices, in general, were medium values. Lucky for me, the quilt shop was across the street, so I could easily add some bright and dark fat quarters.   Decision Making

While I was making approximately 13″ × 13″ pieces of Made-Fabric, I realized that I liked how the yellow and reds were playing off each other. That gave me an idea—I should focus on using a variety of colors, interjecting reds and royal blues as darks and yellows as lights to set it all off.   Risk Taking

Stars are a go-to staple for me. It was a choice I didn't have to think too hard about. I decided to make some simple star blocks using the Made-Fabric in the centers. I cut my pieces and laid them out. (I use a GO! Fabric Cutter by Accuquilt for cutting.) I could see right away that my yellows were singing.   Design

Star blocks for *The Star Splitter* (page 19) before a final layout was determined

As an aside, when I needed a setting fabric for this project, I made a trip to the quilt shop. I wandered all over the large store, but I could not find what I wanted. I avoided the batiks and baby/novelty sections, because I don't usually use these styles of fabrics. In my desperation, however, I finally searched the baby/novelty section, just for kicks. And there (*cue angels singing*) was the perfect yellow-and-pink setting fabric. My lesson from my *aha!* moment? Don't limit your possibilities.   Resourcefulness

---

The Creative Process

Strategy

Decision Making

Risk Taking

Design

Resourcefulness

Tip

Direction is always there—you just need to be open to it. Take a risk!

The Star Splitter, Victoria Findlay Wolfe, 2010, 81″ × 91″

The layout for *The Star Splitter* grew organically through a series of 15-minute play sessions. Personally, I never want to make the same quilt twice, so taking that time to try all the possibilities opens me up to new designs and techniques. In my designs I try to incorporate surprises around the quilt that you might not notice at first glance. Here, I broke up the yellow/pink setting fabric by using four pieces of a different yellow placed in random areas of the border to help draw your eye around the quilt and give your eye a place to rest. Adding the half-square triangle border was a nice way to contain the design. Five half-square triangles are out of order on purpose…. Can you spot them?

Target, Victoria Findlay Wolfe, 2009, 53˝ diameter

While working quickly and outside the box, I played with making fabrics to fit in the circle.

Just Play

To loosen up, work quickly in small blocks of time. Don't think about the outcome; just focus on completing a piece of Made-Fabric—grab, place, sew. Decide later how you will cut up the fabric you've made. The possibilities are endless.

Take one baby step at a time, and stop after each step. Look at how each fabric relates to the one before it. Be aware, make decisions, but move forward quickly. Try not to jump ahead and think about your finished quilt; just focus on what's in front of you. Play and *observe* what you have made. Find something in what you made that makes you smile, and then go with it.

Inspiration can hit at any moment. Blocks made from playing inspire you because you have no idea what they will become. Not knowing is part of the adventure in your creative process.

Get in the habit of asking many questions while you play:

- What am I seeing in what I've made?

- Do I think it is interesting?

- Do I see a color direction that excites me?

- Do I see this being a setting fabric or the block itself?

- How can I approach this in a way I haven't tried before?

Look at your process with new eyes. Focus on ways to try new ideas and techniques. Experiment, put the rules aside, clear your mind, and be open to the possibilities of what you can make from nothing. Trying new things, instead of doing what you *always* do, helps you stay in your creative mind frame and builds confidence in your skills as a quilter.

Beach Houses, LeeAnn Decker,
2010, 43˝ × 26½˝

LeeAnn was cleverly inspired
to turn her Made-Fabric blocks
into little houses for a *two-
sided* wallhanging.

Back of *Beach Houses*.
(Don't forget the back!)

Do you ever get stuck? Sometimes I leave blocks on my wall for weeks. Then, all of a sudden, a solution appears. The answer was right in front of me the whole time; I just wasn't ready to see it before.

NOTE

Don't cross the bridge before you get to it. Here are some ideas if you get stuck in one place.

• Focus on making something from nothing.

• Look for discoveries.

• Decide what your next baby step will be.

• Move forward and stay focused on what you're working on at that moment.

• Trust yourself and try new techniques.

• Relax! Don't worry about mistakes.

Don't worry about getting it wrong. You know you have enough stash to make a lot more quilts. (*Wink!*) Allow yourself to play, to try, without judgment and without fear that you won't know how to proceed. Laugh at your mistakes and pat yourself on the back for learning from them.

Starlight Baby, Victoria Findlay Wolfe, 2010, 32″ × 44″

Using only several lines of Paula Prass fabrics, I made this baby quilt Gwen Marston style, using wonky stars. (Gwen Marston makes glorious, liberated wonky stars by adding slices of fabric at odd angles, giving liberty to traditional patchwork stars.) Then I decided to continue using the Made-Fabric for the sashing. Don't be afraid to try new techniques—you may be surprised at how exciting it is to master a new task!

Staccato, Bonnie Cummings Bus, 2011, 67″ × 76″

Bonnie started out freewheeling these crazy Four-Patch blocks and then incorporated larger pieces of Made-Fabric in her borders. Sometimes the blocks themselves set you off in a wonderful direction, as Bonnie describes: "I sat at the machine and just had to make these blocks. I wanted the center to be a Four-Patch. I wanted the outside to be vaguely like half-square triangles. I couldn't help it—they were calling me, so I came out to play."

Are you afraid to make choices? Why? If you make a mistake, challenge yourself to make it work, as it may be the start of your new favorite quilt. Inspiration is in everything, and there are always more quilts to be made. If you are afraid of making an ugly quilt, you have your energy tied up in the wrong place. You can *always* make another quilt. There are no wrong choices in following your instinct when building a quilt. If you don't try, you won't make discoveries. Lay pieces out and make decisions swiftly. If you're only playing for 15 minutes at a time, how many mistakes can you possibly make?

Boost Your Courage about Using Color

I can show you that you already *know* color, even if you don't think you do. So many people get hung up on color choices. From my own experience, I know that all colors live together just fine.

Here's the secret: If you have color fears, change your thinking.

We all live with color. Every day, we are bombarded with color combinations, color choices, and color patterns. And every day we make conscious decisions about color. We pick out clothes, we paint the walls in our home, and we select fabrics that we have an emotional connection to. Often, we buy fabric solely because we're attracted to it.

Triangles,
Kim Brackett,
2011, 35″ × 45″

Kim found a great solution in using up her small light-colored scraps along with her reds to make this sweet triangles quilt.

You know what you like. You put color together every day by doing what feels right. So, trust that you can also make good choices about color in your quilts. You can get over your fear of color by simply changing your thinking and telling yourself that you can make successful color choices using what you already know. All the information you need, you already have.

Bloomers, Ellen Foster, 2011, 28″ × 20½″

Ellen challenged herself to use Made-Fabric throughout her entire quilt, giving it great movement and its own unique look.

Mixed Paint, Victoria Findlay Wolfe, quilted by Jackie Kunkel, 2010, 52˝ × 62˝

I started this quilt when I received a wonderful piece of Made-Fabric from Gail Norback (top center rectangle). She threw it into a box of fabrics that she was sharing with me, and I couldn't resist using it as a starting point to make this quilt in colors that are way out of my comfort zone. I do love pond-scum green (the name I lovingly call the colors in this quilt), and it forced me to dig out my batiks and play with them. I had pieced some Made-Fabric batik blocks (lower center blue rectangle) a while back, and I knew this new piece from Gail had to live with my old blocks. I tried several layouts, playing randomly to find a way in which they could all live together happily, all the while focusing on the gemlike colors that were inspiring me. When the inspiration hits, I can't ignore it!

BE RESOURCEFUL!

• Use what you have.

• Make what you need.

• Buy cheap!

• Finish pieces that you started but then abandoned.

• Use scraps from other projects.

• Cut up shirts, pants, and kids clothes from your family or thrift stores.

• Create with orphan blocks.

• Use flat bedsheets.

(The American Context #2) Bed Clothes, Luke Haynes, 2010, 96″ × 108″

Luke took found items to another level. Sew them together as you find them! No need for scissors!

Final Thoughts Regarding Play

I am a firm believer that you don't *always* have to know the direction you are going with a quilt. Try to let the possibilities present themselves to you as you play. Make choices as needed, and discover your options as you stumble upon them. Making your own choices, being aware of how you work, and making mistakes are all steps that lead to trusting yourself and your creative process. Being open to what your intuition is telling you and letting your unique quilts evolve is a very exciting adventure!

Allow the process to work for you, so you can create a quilt that is made, designed, and born from your own creative journey. Don't make quilts that look like mine; make quilts that look like yours. Use these techniques as a way to jump-start your own creative path. If you open your eyes to new possibilities, you will feel more confident in your fabric choices, design elements, and overall aesthetic by knowing you've built a quilt from nothing into something that is very personal and very you.

Four Easy Techniques for "Made-Fabric"

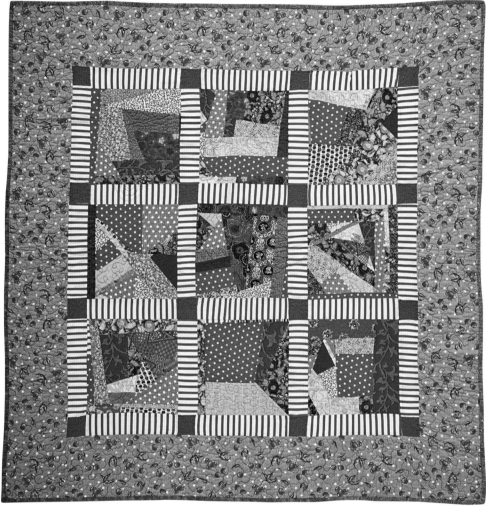

Crazy Beanz, Victoria Findlay Wolfe, 2009, 57″ × 57″

Under my sewing table, I keep a big clear bin to collect small scraps. I toss in scraps as I sew, and I sift through the bin when I want to play and make fabric.

Sewing scraps together is not a new concept. I relish the fact that it is a way to make something similar to my grandmother's quilts. When I find even older quilts made the same way, I feel a real bond to the quilts and the quilters who made them. Their purpose was solely necessity—the quilters used what they had. Today, I can relate to that theory of waste not, want not. Use what you have. That is what feeds my play.

Made-Fabric is created by taking bits of otherwise useless scraps and sewing them together to make a usable piece of fabric that can then be utilized to make a variety of blocks and quilts. It's a chance to make something from nothing that might otherwise not have found a home in a quilt.

Fragment II, Dorothy LeBoeuf, 2011, 14½″ × 17¾″

Free-Pieced Made-Fabric

Mini Pineapples, Victoria Findlay Wolfe, 2011, 16″ × 16″

Got your scrap bins?

Get ready to jump in!

Ready, steady, jump!

Tips

• *If you are a beginner, or if having straight edges on your scraps will help you have straight seams, then trim the edges straight.*

Straight seams = Flat blocks

• *Use a small stitch length when making fabric to keep the seams from pulling apart.*

---

1. Start by selecting a handful of scraps (Figure 1). Try to refrain from cleaning up the edges, unless you feel you really need to. If you can accomplish straight seams without cutting a straight edge as a guideline, then go for it—nobody is watching.

2. Either lay out the scraps in a planned way, or just pick up a scrap and sew a second scrap onto one of its straight edges (Figure 2).

3. Trim the seam allowance to ¼″. I prefer to sew and then cut. I can make most fabric with just my scissors—no rotary cutter.

4. Press the seam allowances in one direction (Figure 3).

5. Keep adding bits of fabric—on and around, here and there—pressing as you add each piece (Figures 4 and 5). You can use as many or as few scraps as you like. Using fewer larger pieces makes blocks faster, whereas

many smaller pieces may make more interesting blocks. Stop when you feel it's big enough or if it's getting difficult to add more.

6. Later, when you decide what you want to make with this fabric, trim the fabric to the exact size you need (Figures 6, 7, and 8).

Try following these steps for just 15 minutes. Making Made-Fabric is like eating potato chips—you can't eat (make) just one!

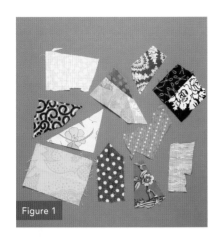

Figure 1

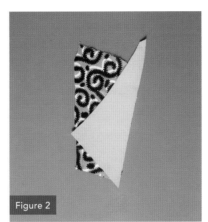

Figure 2

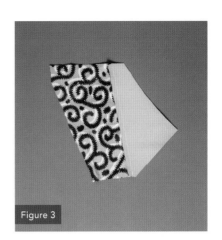

Figure 3

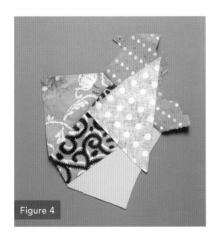

Figure 4

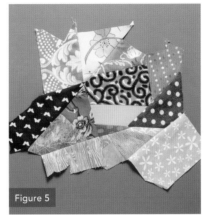

Figure 5

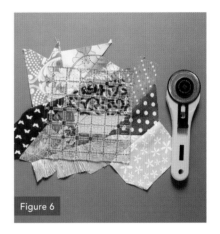

Figure 6

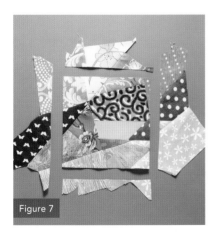

Figure 7

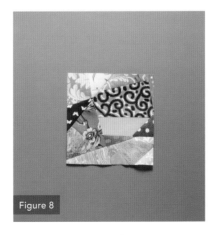

Figure 8

Tips

• You don't always have to follow your raw edge. I try to incorporate as many varied angles as possible and stay away from 90° angles (hard angles) whenever possible. Otherwise the result will be a very linear block

• Bonus bits are the pieces of two or more pieced fabrics that you have cut off from a previous piece of Made-Fabric. Add them to a new piece of Made-Fabric or use them to start your next morsel of Made-Fabric.

• If an added piece makes it difficult to add another bit, cut it off to make a fresh straight edge. Start piecing a separate bit of Made-Fabric, trim it to make a straight edge, and join it to your in-progress piece.

• Focus on:

Angles—*the more, the merrier.*

Prints with curves—*they give great movement to a block.*

Wild prints—*they will help create the illusion of a crazy-quilt block and will easily blend your hard angles.*

Incorporate as many or as few of these ideas as you play.

• *Don't* focus on:

Making a square block—*Let the fabric take you on its own journey. Just make the fabric!*

Sew.

Cut.

Sew again!

Make friends with your scissors.

Don't like a bit? Cut it off.

Save it for the next piece!

Grandiflora, Rachaeldaisy, 2011, 74″ × 74″

Rachaeldaisy added a large border of Made-Fabric around her beautiful medallion center. You do not always have to cut up your Made-Fabric. Leaving it in large pieces can give your quilt a very *grand* look!

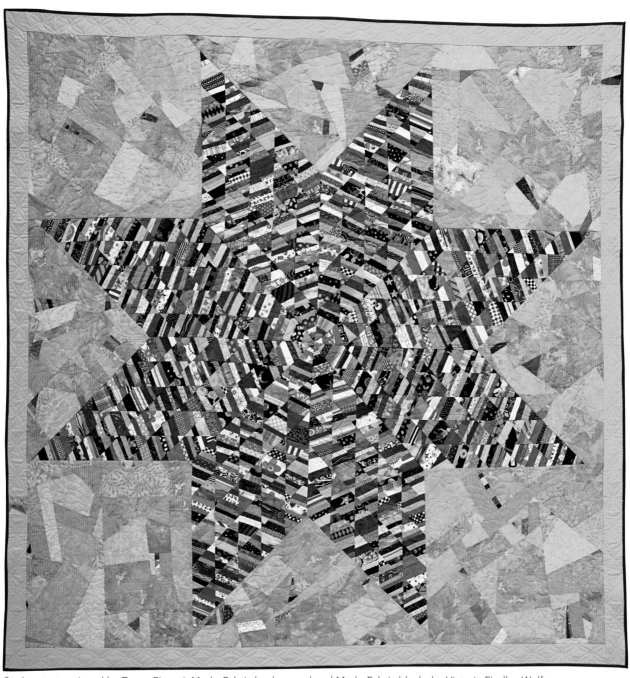

Starburst, star pieced by Tonya Ricucci, Made-Fabric background and Made-Fabric blocks by Victoria Findlay Wolfe, quilted by Jackie Kunkel, 2011, 73″ × 73″

I used Tonya's scraps from her pieced star to incorporate into the Made-Fabric setting for this collaborative quilt.

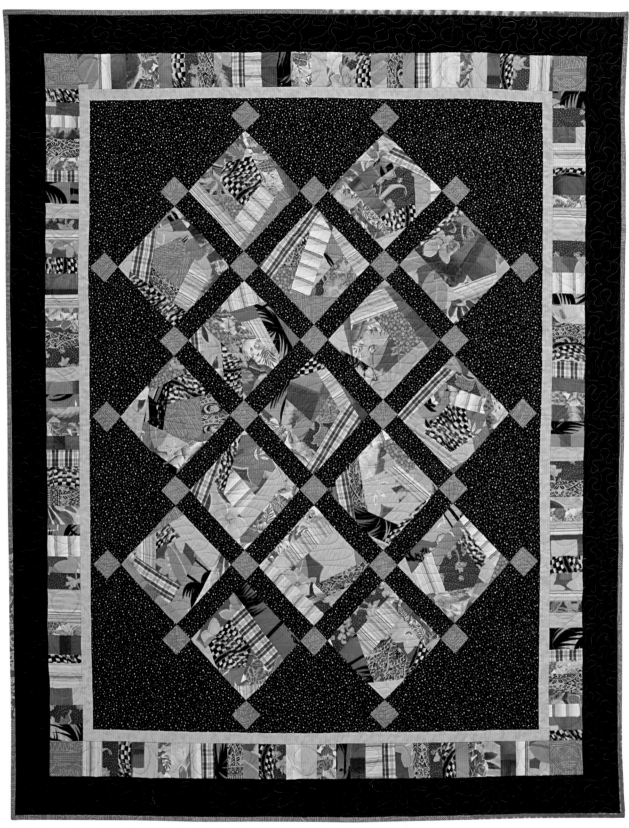

Shirts Gone Crazy, Patty House, quilted by Carol Graves, 2011, 60″ × 75″

Patty made a unique original design by letting the sashing around her Made-Fabric blocks blend into the background.

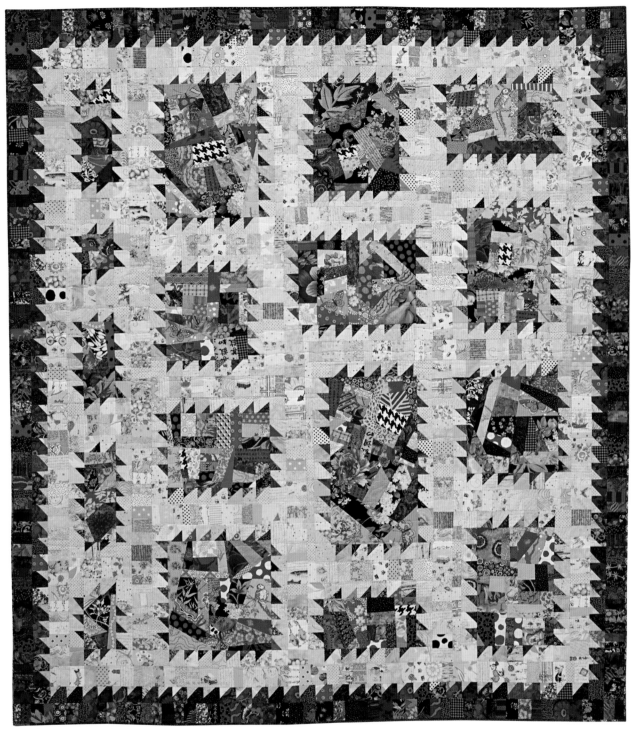

Rendezvous, Karen Griska, 2011, 78˝ × 87˝

Karen started with random-sized Made-Fabric blocks. Later she went back, decided on the layout, and planned to keep the setting as scrappy as possible.

Paper-Pieced Made-Fabric

Moody Blues, Victoria Findlay Wolfe, quilted by Jackie Kunkel, 2011, 79″ × 83″

With *Moody Blues*, I was determined to make a blue quilt. I seem to have more blues than any other color in my stash, yet I never make blue quilts. It was great to clean out my stash bins of blue scraps. I started with a 6″ × 12″ piece of phone-book paper. Using a ruler that size made for easy trimming later.

Use phone-book paper as a guide when you are trying to make a particular size of a block. It's lightweight, which means the paper will tear away easily.

Start with a **small stitch length** on your sewing machine (smaller than for regular piecing) to keep your seams from coming apart when you trim your block to size.

1. Cut the phone-book paper to the block size you want.

2. Place a scrap right side up so it *covers* the edge of the paper. Place a second scrap on top of the first scrap, right

sides together, aligning a straight edge (Figure 1).

3. Sew a ¼″ seam through the paper and fabrics.

NOTE

If you are using oddly shaped pieces, trim the edge straight, or sew the straight seamline and then trim off the odd bit (with scissors), keeping your seam allowance ¼″ wide.

4. Fold open and press.

5. Add the next piece, right sides together, along another straight edge.

6. Fold open and press (Figure 2).

7. Continue adding new pieces, right sides together and folding open and pressing (Figure 3), until you've covered the entire piece of paper (Figure 4).

8. Remove the paper (Figure 5).*

9. Press the block and trim to your desired block size (Figure 6).

*I leave the paper in place when cutting shapes such as diamonds that will later be pieced into a quilt using a Y-seam. The paper adds stability.

Tip

Try to add pieces at varying angles. The more varied angles you incorporate, the more interesting your block will be.

Making a whole bunch of these blocks will give you something fun to play with later, when you create the design.

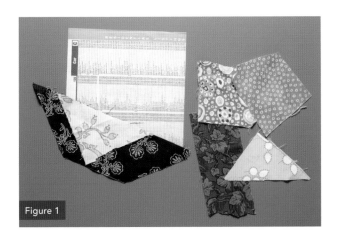

Figure 1

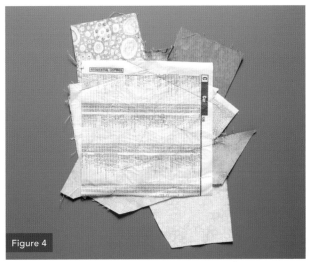

Figure 4

Figure 2

Figure 5

Figure 3

Figure 6

Tree of Life, Karen Griska, 2005, 64″ × 64″

The overall movement that happens when using paper-pieced Made-Fabric throughout an entire quilt gives amazing depth to the piece and leads to a completely unique creation.

Diamond Garden, Victoria Findlay Wolfe, quilted by Angela Walters, 2011, 86″ × 105″

My goal with this quilt was to make scrappy flowers growing from a patch of earth. Paper piecing my Made-Fabric was a good choice when piecing the Y-seams for these blocks. The foundation keeps the pieces stable when pivoting to join Y-seams. Once I made the blocks and removed the foundation paper, I embroidered around each flower and stem for an added element to be discovered when wrapped up in this quilt.

Five-Sided Made-Fabric

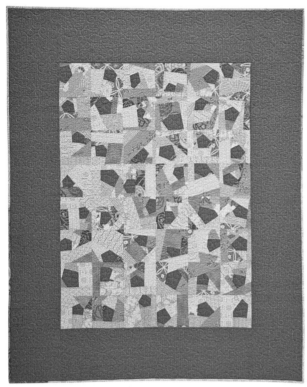

Little Brick Houses, Donna Mae Elfering, quilted by Jackie Kunkel, 2011, 53″ × 65″

Donna cut completely random five-sided shapes before she started adding her aqua blue scraps around each shape. She went back afterward and cut the blocks down to the size she wanted. Then she played with the arrangement until they danced around in a free-spirited way.

I love playing with this technique. It is based on a traditional crazy quilt block, which uses a central starter shape. Judith Baker Montano calls it the centerpiece method in her books. Any number of sides will work, but I like the effect of five sides. Just add pieces around the center shape. You can make the block any size—just keep adding scraps of fabric.

1. Start with a bold-colored, 5-sided scrap (Figure 1).

2. Place a scrap right sides together on a straight edge of the first shape. Don't worry if the scrap is big or little—the more variety there is, the more interesting the block will be.

3. Sew the seam. Trim the seam allowance if necessary.

4. Flip the piece open and press (Figure 2).

5. Place a rotary cutting ruler over the next straight edge and trim the scrap fabric even with the next straight side of the center. Doing so will guarantee that the block will lay flat.

6. Align the next scrap right sides together with the straight edge trimmed in Step 5. Make sure the new scrap is long enough to cover the straight edge of the center and the first piece. Sew the seam and trim the seam allowance, if needed.

7. Open the pieces, and press (Figure 3).

8. Repeat Steps 5–7 around the block, any way you like (Figure 4), until you have a piece slightly larger than the block size you need; press (Figures 5).

9. Trim to the unfinished block size (Figures 6 and 7).

> ### Tip
> *You can use single or pieced scraps for the added pieces. For a very random scrappy look, sew the scraps into strips, adding them to the center and trimming as instructed. Save trimmed bits or pieces of Made-Fabric. The more angles you incorporate, the more interesting your block becomes.*

I often like to make larger pieces of Made-Fabric. With larger pieces, I can lay my ruler exactly over a piece that I want to cut out in a precise way. I can also cut more than one piece from a large piece of Made-Fabric.

Tips

• Remember! If you don't like it, cut it off.

• If your block will not lie flat, cut off the bit that is being unruly. You will find that it will lie flat once it's been cut. Cool!

• Be sure to use a small stitch length when making fabric.

Cut, sew, cut, sew, and cut again!

The beauty of scraps is that you always have more.

Keep going and keep trying new things.

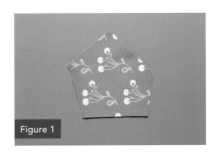

Figure 1

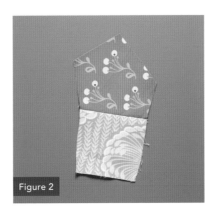

Figure 2

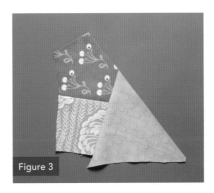

Figure 3

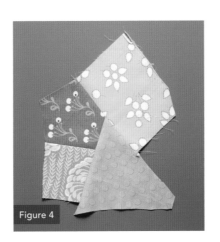

Figure 4

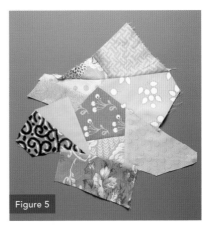

Figure 5

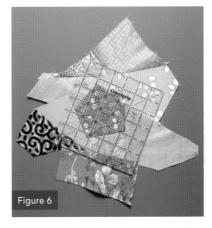

Figure 6

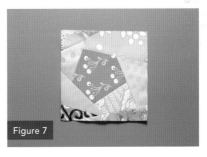

Figure 7

Crazy Scraps, LeeAnn Decker, 2010, 84″ × 84″

LeeAnn worked quickly as she added scraps around a central shape. Her amazing color palette makes a playground for inspirational discoveries. When you look into each block, can you find color combinations that you like? What discoveries can you find that may lead you to your next quilt?

Weekend Scrapper, Victoria Findlay Wolfe, 2010, 70″ × 91″

This is an example of five-sided piecing and following your instincts.

The Weekend Scrapper Experiment

After I made some 13″ blocks using the five-sided technique and laid them out, I was curious about what would happen if I cut them into half-square triangles—I do love half-square triangles. Since there are no mistakes and I can always make more blocks, I happily sliced 12 blocks in half. This is a great scrap-buster quilt! I wanted the quilt to be bed size, so I added a perimeter row of blocks as a border using one-fabric triangles made from many of the same fabrics that I had used in the pieced triangles. This quilt is a perfect example of not having a set idea when starting a quilt.

Let the fabrics and blocks speak to you. Ask "What if …?" Then follow your instinct to make an original and unique quilt. In *Weekend Scrapper*, I let the fabrics and blocks tell me the direction in which the quilt wanted to go. What I thought would be a great big scrappy-block quilt quickly turned a corner and became a fun, happy, scrappy weekend quilt.

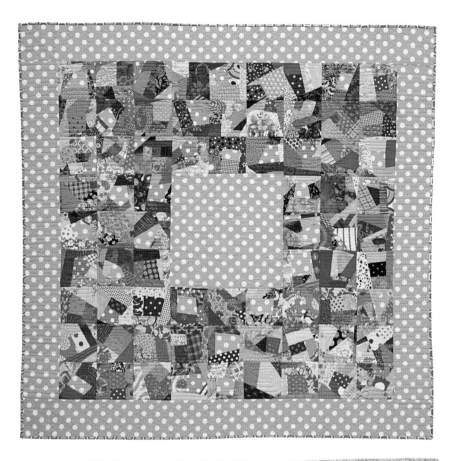

Polka Dots Squared, Victoria Findlay Wolfe, quilted by Angela Walters, 2011, 57″ × 59″

Using a four-sided shape to make Made-Fabric, it was the dots that inspired the layout for this quilt, as described in Why 15 Minutes? (page 15).

Sweet September, Beth Shibley, 2011, 39″ × 41″

Beth's primary-color palette and use of vintage fabrics set a nice "already been loved" tone for this sweet baby quilt.

Fast-and-Easy Made-Fabric

J Rock Star, Victoria Findlay Wolfe, quilted by Jackie Kunkel, 2011, 65˝ × 66˝

Using a line of Jay McCarroll Habitat fabrics, I cut random squares and rectangles to make fast-and-easy fabric. I then slashed in strips of red Kona cotton and used my giant template to cut the parallelograms for the star sections.

Having a need to make something quickly one day, I wondered, *What if* (a very important question to ask when playing) *I cut or pieced a bunch of 6½˝ × 6½˝ squares, sewed them together, and then used a template to trim them to my desired shape?* With this technique, I found a great way to make big, impressive, quick quilts.

You can also try combining 6½˝ × 6½˝ blocks with 12½˝ × 12½˝ blocks or any combination of sizes that will allow you to join them quickly and give you a variety of patterns.

1. Place the pieces or blocks on a design wall in an arrangement that looks right to you (Figure 1).

2. Sew them together into a large piece of fabric (Figures 2 and 3).

3. Trim the pieces using a template (Figure 4). Cutting 8 pieces will make one big beautiful star (Figure 5).

You can use this technique to cut almost any shape that makes up a quilt block.

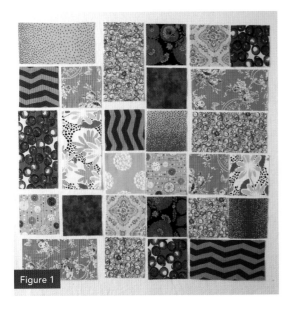

Figure 1

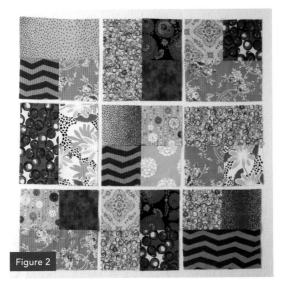

Figure 2

Figure 3

Figure 4

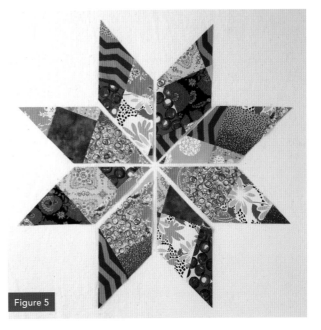

Figure 5

Barn Star, Victoria Findlay Wolfe, quilted by Jackie Kunkel, 2011, 95″ × 95″

I used the fast-and-easy technique (page 44) to create the diamonds for this quilt. I sewed eight identical sets of squares (Figure A); then I cut eight matching diamonds (Figure B) to achieve the star's visual balance.

Figure A

Figure B

Summer Samba, Bonnie Cummings Bus, quilted by Angela Walters, 2011, 62″ × 62″

Using a large template to cut her stars from Made-Fabrics, Bonnie went about creating her own unique quilt with fun, quirky colors.

16 Quilt Blocks
to Get You Inspired

Let the blocks in this chapter inspire you. Create Made-Fabric using one of the piecing techniques from Four Easy Techniques for "Made-Fabric" (page 28). Then use the instructions on the following pages to create 12″ × 12″ finished blocks of your choice.

Half-Square Triangle

Made-Fabric:
Use any technique.

Cut 1 square 12⅞″ × 12⅞″; cut in half diagonally to make 2 half-square triangles (A). (You will use 1 triangle for each block.)

Solid fabric:
Cut 1 square 12⅞″ × 12⅞″; cut in half diagonally to make 2 half-square triangles (B). (You will use 1 triangle for each block.)

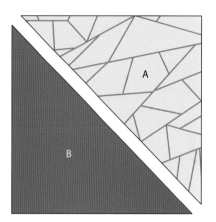

Sawtooth Star

Made-Fabric:
Use any technique.

Cut 1 square 6½″ × 6½″ (A).

Star points:
Use Made-Fabric or a variety of fabrics.

Cut 4 squares 3⅞″ × 3⅞″; cut in half diagonally to make 8 half-square triangles (B).

Background fabric:
Cut 4 squares 3½″ × 3½″ (C).

Cut 1 square 7¼″ × 7¼″; cut in half diagonally in both directions to make 4 quarter-square triangles (D).

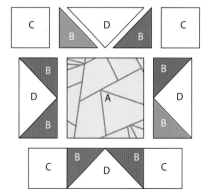

Mod Strips

Made-Fabric:

Use any technique—I used the paper-pieced technique (page 36).

Cut 2 strips 3½″ × 12½″ (A).

Solid fabric:

Cut 2 strips 3½″ × 12½″ (B).

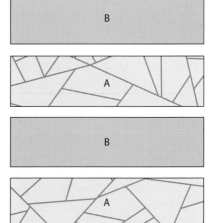

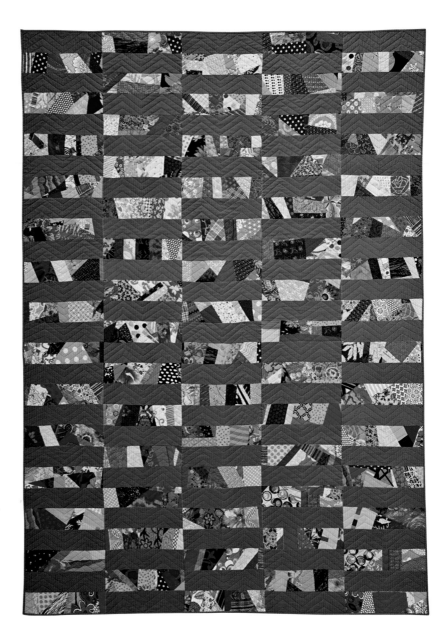

Making Me Crazy, Victoria Findlay Wolfe, quilted by Shelly Pagliai, 2011, 59″ × 82″

In this modern twin-size quilt, the Made-Fabric is showcased nicely by the gray slate fabric.

Giant Whirlygigs

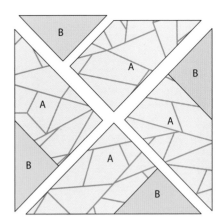

Made-Fabric:

Use any technique—I used the paper-pieced technique (page 36).

1. Cut 2 strips 4¾″ × 14¼″.

2. Measure along the top edge 4¾″ from the left corner and make a mark. Measure 4¾″ along the bottom edge from the right corner and make a mark. Cut a 45° angle connecting the 2 marks to make 2 wedges.

3. Repeat Step 2 with the remaining strip to make a total of 4 wedges (A).

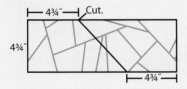

Background fabric:

Cut 1 square 7¼″ × 7¼″; cut in half diagonally in both directions to make 4 quarter-square triangles (B).

Whirlygigs Galore, Victoria Findlay Wolfe and Donna Mae Elfering, quilted by Shelly Pagliai, 2011, 59″ × 83″

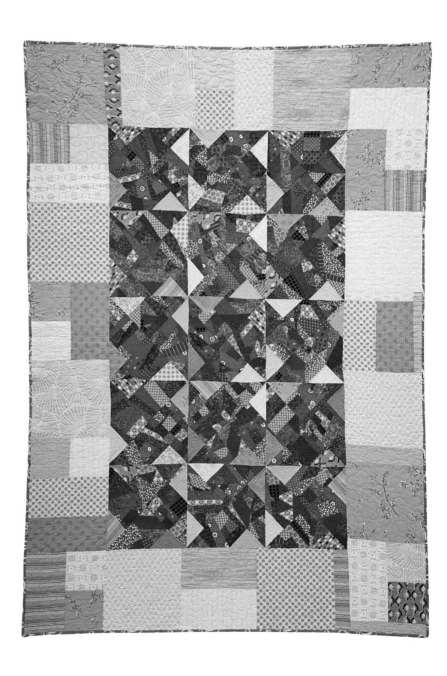

After making the Giant Whirlygigs blocks, I used the fast-and-easy technique (page 44) to add a scrappy border around the quilt in light blues. Using this method dresses up the border and gives it a bit more depth than it would have had with one simple fabric.

X Marks the Spot

Made-Fabric:

Use any technique.

Cut 5 squares 4¾″ × 4¾″ (A).

Background fabric:

Cut 1 square 7¼″ × 7¼″; cut in half diagonally in both directions to make 4 quarter-square triangles (B).

Cut 2 squares 3⅞″ × 3⅞″; cut in half diagonally to make 4 half-square triangles (C).

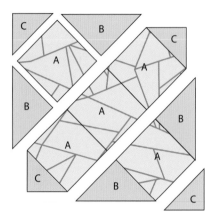

Lady Fingers

Made-Fabric:

Use any technique.

Cut 4 squares 2⅞″ × 2⅞″; cut in half diagonally to make 8 half-square triangles (A).

Cut 4 squares 2½″ × 2½″ (B).

Cut 1 square 4½″ × 4½″ (C).

Background fabric:

Cut 4 squares 4½″ × 4½″ (D).

Cut 4 squares 2½″ × 2½″ (E).

Cut 4 squares 2⅞″ × 2⅞″; cut in half diagonally to make 8 half-square triangles (F).

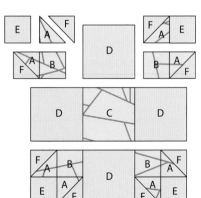

Scrapped Shoo Fly

Made-Fabric:

Use any technique.

Cut 1 square 4½″ × 4½″ (A).

Cut 2 squares 4⅞″ × 4⅞″; cut in half diagonally to make 4 half-square triangles (B).

Background fabric:

Cut 2 squares 4⅞″ × 4⅞″; cut in half diagonally to make 4 half-square triangles (C).

Cut 4 squares 4½″ × 4½″ (D).

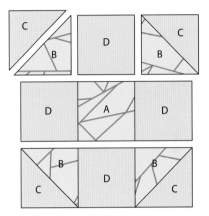

Split Square

Made-Fabric:

Use any technique.

Cut 1 square 6½″ × 6½″ (A).

Solid fabric:

Cut 4 rectangles 1½″ × 3½″ (B).

Background fabric:

Cut 8 rectangles 3½″ × 3″ (C).

Cut 4 squares 3½″ × 3½″ (D).

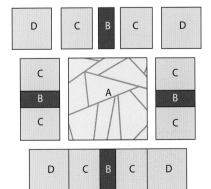

Square in a Square, Squared

Made-Fabric:

Use any technique—I used the five-sided technique (page 40).

Cut 1 square 6½″ × 6½″ (A).

Inner-triangle fabric:
Cut 2 squares 5⅛″ × 5⅛″; cut in half diagonally to make 4 half-square triangles (B).

Outer-triangle fabric:
Cut 2 squares 6⅞″ × 6⅞″; cut in half diagonally to make 4 half-square triangles (C).

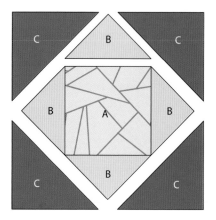

Elda's Flower

Made-Fabric:
Use any technique.

Cut 1 square 11¼″ × 11¼″; cut in half diagonally in both directions to make 4 quarter-square triangles (C).

Solid fabrics:

Cut 1 square 2″ × 2″ (A).

Cut 4 strips 2″ × 8½″ (B).

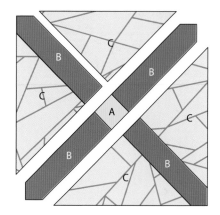

Scrap Star

Made-Fabric:

Use any technique.

Cut 3 squares 5¼″ × 5¼″; cut in half diagonally in both directions to make 12 quarter-square triangles (A).

Background fabric:

Cut 1 square 5¼″ × 5¼″; cut in half diagonally in both directions to make 4 quarter-square triangles (B).

Cut 5 squares 4½″ × 4½″ (C).

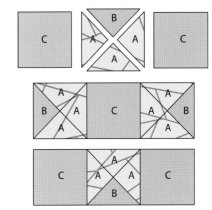

Sawtooth Square

Made-Fabric:

Use any technique.

Cut 1 square 6½″ × 6½″ (A).

Print fabric:

Cut 4 squares 3⅞″ × 3⅞″; cut in half diagonally to make 8 half-square triangles (B).

Background fabric:

Cut 4 squares 3⅞″ × 3⅞″; cut in half diagonally to make 8 half-square triangles (C).

Cut 4 squares 3½″ × 3½″ (D).

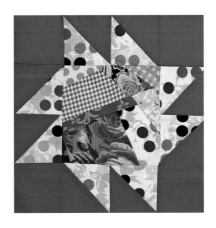

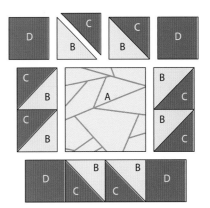

LeMoyne Star

Made-Fabric:

Use any technique.

1. Cut 2 strips 2½″ × 21½″.

2. Measure 2½″ along the bottom edge and cut a 45° angle from the top left corner to this mark. Discard the small triangle of Made-Fabric or use it in another project.

3. Make another 45° angle cut 4¾″ from the cut in Step 2. Repeat to cut a total of 4 parallelograms (A) from the strip. Discard the remaining small triangle or use it in another project.

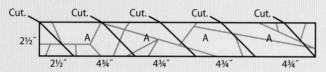

4. Measure 2½″ along the *top* edge of the remaining 2½″ × 21½″ strip and cut from the bottom left corner to this mark. Do not use the small triangle in this block.

5. Make a parallel cut 4¾″ from the cut in Step 4. Repeat to cut a total of 4 parallelograms (Ar) from the strip. Do not use the leftover small triangle in this block.

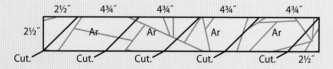

Background fabric:

Cut 1 square 5¼″ × 5¼″; cut in half diagonally in both directions to make 4 quarter-square triangles (B).

Cut 4 squares 4½″ × 4½″ (C).

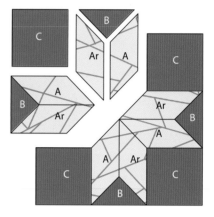

Y-Seams

NOTE

Change Your Thinking about Y-Seams

Think of Y-seams as a simple pivot, instead of as "the dreaded Y-seam." Learning this trick will provide you with a useful technique to facilitate making more interesting quilt blocks and Made-Fabric. Take 15 minutes to play with Y-seams. Once you master them, you will have a valuable tool to create unique quilts.

1. With right sides together, place a triangle on a parallelogram as shown. Sew using a ¼˝ seam allowance, stopping ¼˝ before the end of the fabric. Backstitch and cut the threads. Press the seam open.

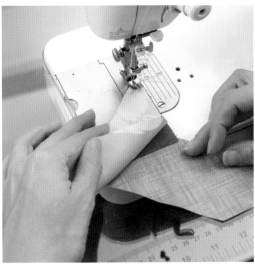

2. With right sides together, place the next parallelogram on top of the right edge of the triangle. Sew with a ¼˝ seam allowance and stop with the needle in the down position when you reach the seam where the first 2 pieces meet.

3. With the needle down, pivot the top and bottom pieces so the edges line up. Continue sewing to the outer edge.

4. Press the seams open to reveal a beautiful Y-seam!

Flying Geese

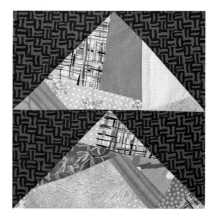

Made-Fabric:

Use any technique.

Cut 1 square 9⅜″ × 9⅜″; cut in half diagonally to make 2 half-square triangles (A).

Background fabric:

Cut 2 squares 6⅞″ × 6⅞″; cut in half diagonally to make 4 half-square triangles (B).

Slashing

Made-Fabric:

Use any technique.

Cut 1 square 12½″ × 12½″ (A).

Strips:

Cut a variety 1″- to 2″-wide strips (B and C).

1. Place the ruler over the fabric at a random angle and cut the block from edge to edge.

2. Sew the block back together, placing one of the strips from Step 1 (B) between the block halves.

3. Place the ruler over the block at a different angle and cut from edge to edge again.

4. Continue adding as many strips (C) into the block as you like.

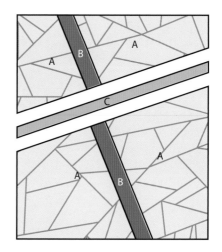

Twister

Made-Fabric:

Use any technique.

Cut 4 squares 6½″ × 6½″ (A).

Print fabric:

Cut 4 strips 3½″ × 6½″ (B).

1. On a Made-Fabric square (A), measure in 1¾″ from the top right corner and 2¾″ from the bottom right corner, and make a cut connecting those two points. Use the larger piece; save the smaller piece for a future project.

2. Place the print strip over the edge cut in Step 2; sew.

3. Trim the unit to 6½″ × 6½″.

4. Repeat Steps 1–3 to make 4 units. Arrange as shown in the block photo (at right).

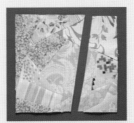

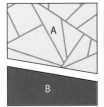

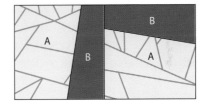

Lucky's Cloud, Victoria Findlay Wolfe,
2011, 39″ × 44½″

Using Made-Fabric, the LeMoyne
Star block, and the word *cloud* for
inspiration, baby Lucky gets a cloud
of his own to sleep under.

Crazy Geese, Beth Shibley with
15 Minute Scrap Bee block contribu-
tors: LeeAnn Decker, Glenda Parks,
Sujata Shaw, Margaret Cibulsky,
Shelly Pagliai, Charlotte Pountney,
Mary Ramsey Keasler, Helen Beall,
Brenda Suderman, Lynn O'Brien, and
Victoria Findlay Wolfe, 2011, 72″ × 73″

NOTE

On my website, www.15minutesplay.com, I ran a quilting bee called 15 Minute Scrap Bee, which included twelve participants. Each person was assigned a month, and each made a tutorial for a block that uses Made-Fabric. In *Crazy Geese* (page 60), Beth made a tutorial for making Crazy Geese blocks. Each of the other eleven people made the Crazy Geese blocks and sent them to Beth. When she had all of her blocks, she created her quilt. Margaret Cibulsky's *No Schema* (below) came from the same quilting bee. A quilting bee is a fun way to create outside the box.

No Schema, Margaret Cibulsky with 15 Minute Scrap Bee block contributors: LeeAnn Decker, Glenda Parks, Sujata Shaw, Shelly Pagliai, Charlotte Pountney, Mary Ramsey Keasler, Helen Beall, Brenda Suderman, Beth Shibley, Lynn O'Brien and Victoria Findlay Wolfe, 2011, 52″ × 63″

These fun blocks were requested by Margaret in the 15 Minute Scrap Bee. Margaret used Made-Fabric as a start for the block and added slashing through each block for contrast. Next, she carried the slashing out into the borders to make a complete thought and a unique, beautiful quilt.

Double Crossroads, Bonnie Cummings Bus, 2011, 42″ × 53½″

Bonnie used slashing as a technique, not just in her block design, but also in the entire layout of the quilt.

11 Challenges to Get You Going

Get Thrifty!

> **CHALLENGE #1**
>
> *Make a quilt entirely from clothing.*

An oldie idea, but a goodie!

People have been making quilts from clothing out of necessity for ages. Now the necessity is that we're going green—use what you have!

Consider making quilts from those soft, luscious-but-outdated cotton garments you couldn't bear to get rid of. And while you are at it, why stop at cottons? Buy a variety of fabrics on sale at thrift shops. My grandmother made quilts from left-over double knits, and I can tell you, they are still warm and in very good shape!

15 Minutes to Play and Contemplate

Plaids, stripes, uniforms, suits, sheets …

Sweaters, T-shirts …

Jeans, flannel …

Upholstery fabrics …

What do you have that can be cut up and repurposed? Is anything off-limits?

Are you making a memory quilt? Using what you have lends itself nicely to memory quilts. Has your child outgrown her favorite clothes? Has your hubby sent his work shirts to the dry cleaners a few too many times? Do you still have your rock band T-shirt collection from the 1980s? Using the fabrics around you can make nice memories—and even nicer quilts!

Sunday Best, Mary Ramsey Keasler, 2011, 72″ × 84″

Mary started this quilt by using her daughters' cotton-flannel shirts. She had a "work clothes" color scheme in mind. Not pleased with the results, she put the top away for a year. When she pulled it out later, she decided to "dress it up in its Sunday Best" by using 15 minutes of play to make flowers from her scraps. After several attempts with the layout, she finished her quilt. Her play and patience really paid off.

Stripes Plaids and Polka Dots, Victoria Findlay Wolfe, quilted by Angela Walters, 2011, 86″ × 91″

Blocks of striped, plaid, and polka-dot Made-Fabric were donated to me by participants of my "15 Minutes Play" website. I pieced the stars and block borders with the Made-Fabric and used thrift store shirtings for the background. I let the variety of fabrics in the stars guide my color palette. Wanting to capitalize on the dots and patterns, I appliquéd the large black dots and the zigzag around the quilt for some added *zing*!

Gifts #18 Alliances, Luke Haynes,
2011, 17½″ × 17½″

Luke used a variety of fabrics, from
polyester and fleece to cotton. He often
goes to the thrift store to choose clothing
sorted by color, and he buys it by the
pound.

Transitions, Margaret Cibulsky,
2006–2010, 49″ × 75″

Margaret used her late husband's clothing
as a starting point for this memory quilt. She
cut up the clothing to make simple blocks
that had memories attached to them. The
Burberry plaid was from his raincoat, the
binding was from a shirt he always wore
to chemo, and the black-and-white tweed
was from a skirt he had given Margaret
twenty years ago that she had never
worn. Margaret embroidered a detail of
three pussy willows, something she always
brought into the house in the spring—one
for herself, and one for each of her sons.
This quilt is her way to show looking forward
while also remembering her memories. She
also used the slashing technique (page 58)
to add interest in the borders.

Scrap Swap!

CHALLENGE #2

Force yourself to use every last bit of fabric your scrap partner sends you.

Wait, hold that scrap!

Don't throw anything away!

Too small for you? Tired of that print you've used in twenty quilts? Throw it into a bag and save it. Later do a scrap swap with another quilter, because one quilter's trash is another quilter's treasure!

Seeing what someone else buys can really spark your creativity as well. Look at how their choices differ from yours.

What do you like in the new stash?

Is there something there that is missing from your own stash?

If you don't like your partner's scraps, then you have another challenge. How can you make them interesting and into something you like?

15 Minutes to Play and Contemplate

Time your layout. See how quickly you can lay it all out into something that pleases you. Then step back and look at it for 15 minutes.

Ask a lot of questions: What's working? What's not? What can you add to the design to make it interesting? Try using every bit of fabric.

Blue Geese, Victoria Findlay Wolfe, 2009, 21″ × 21″, scraps donated by Ellen Foster

Ellen gave me a bag of scraps, and the challenge was to use everything I was given. I incorporated many techniques all in one small quilt—curves, Made-Fabric, appliqué, and reverse appliqué. Then, I had fun with straight-line and free-motion quilting.

Scrap Exchange Quilt, Bonnie Cummings Bus,
2010, 36½″ × 40½″

I sent Bonnie a bag of my scraps, and she
used them basically as she found them,
randomly pulling pieces and sewing them
together. She hand-quilted it with big
undulating circles to add another great
element to the quilt.

All Mine, Victoria Findlay Wolfe and Kathie Holland,
machine quilted by Lorre Fleming, 2009, 49½″ × 56″

In early 2009, I decided I was tired of my scraps. I felt
as if I were constantly using the same colors and prints
over and over. So I asked on my blog whether anyone
wanted my scraps. Kathie said yes, and I quickly
sent her a box of fabrics. Once I saw the super-cute
tumblers she was making from my scraps, I felt very
emotional. I saw fabrics I had used to make my daughter's bedding, and clothes I had made for my daughter
and others—all on Kathie's website. Knowing I was so
sentimental about the fabrics, Kathie very kindly sent
me what became the middle panel of this quilt. I was
so touched by this that I decided I would finish it off
with my favorite fabrics. Then I named it *All Mine.* I
learned my lesson—savor those scraps. *Wink!*

Solids and Prints

CHALLENGE #3

Mix solids and prints.

One day in my early days of obsessive quilting, as I left my friend Tonya's house, she leaned out the door and yelled after me, "Use more solids!" The thought had never occurred to me to mix the solids and prints.

I had no solids in my stash, so I went home and ordered a bunch. Then I went to town cutting them up and sewing them back together. Using all solids can be fun, but what if you mix them with prints? Which one will be your inspiration—the solids or the prints?

15 Minutes to Play and Contemplate

Find inspiration around you. For 15 minutes, walk around your home and find things that inspire you to make a quilt.

Is it a shirt you own?

Your china pattern?

A color scheme in your house?

Think about how you can balance solids and prints to make something modern or traditional.

In One Way, Daniel Rouse, 2011, 58″ × 78″

Daniel is great at curved piecing. He took a scrappy background quilt and made it something special by adding in some solids to bring it all together.

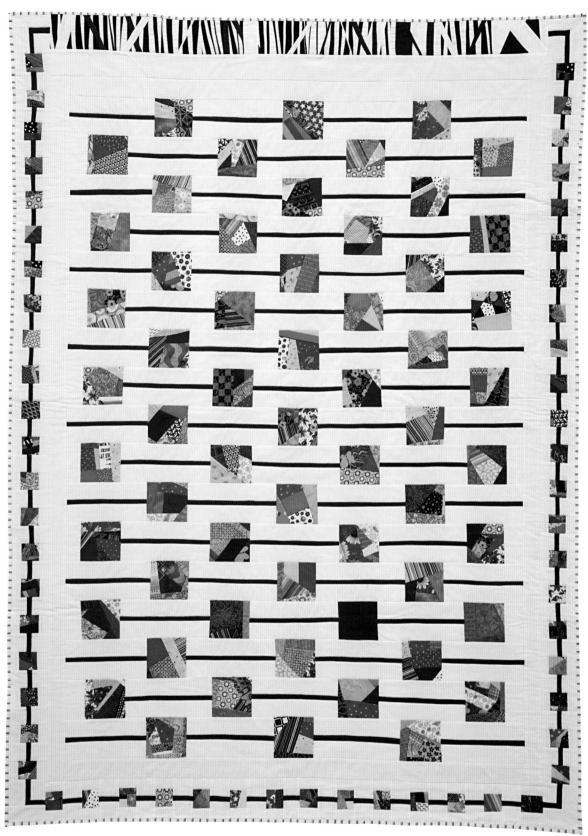

Indications of Rhythm, Margaret Cibulsky, 2010–2011, 56½˝ × 72˝

Margaret played with many layouts before settling on this playful dance of Made-Fabric blocks. Stay connected to your 15-minute process—take 15 minutes, whenever you can, to try new things. Your first thought does not need to be your only thought. Consider all the options through your play.

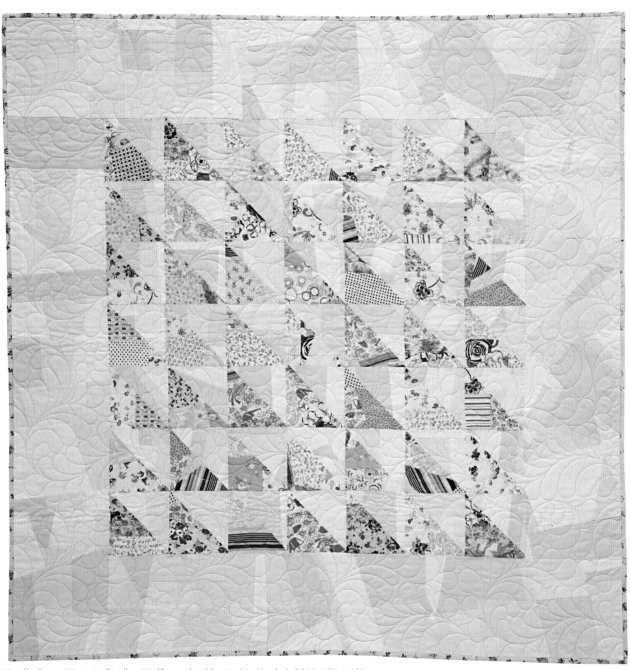

Vanilla Bean, Victoria Findlay Wolfe, quilted by Jackie Kunkel, 2011, 49″ × 49″

I have never been fond of white fabrics, but I found that making this quilt opened my eyes to the beauty of light-ish prints. Using the different solid tones and values of white, beige, and pink and mixing them into Made-Fabrics gave this baby quilt just the softest touch of "sweet" that it needed in its borders!

Cool and Warm Colors

Warm and cool colors. How do you define them?

Do you look at the color chart and pick them literally, or do you have a sense of a warm color and a cool color that relates to you?

I have found that some people have different views about what is warm and what is cool, depending on what they personally associate the color with.

Typically, blues, purples, and greens are cool, while red, orange, and yellow are warm.

Pick two warm colors and two cool colors and make a quilt that blends them in one coherent design.

I used to dislike purple and gold together, because they were our school colors…

"Here's to the victors bold, the purple and the gold! Go Dutchmen!"

I found it a huge challenge to make something appealing to *my* eye using purple and gold. But, after using this color palette a few times, I think I have two new favorite colors. Go figure!

15 Minutes to Play and Contemplate

Which two colors do you not like together? Often they will be a warm and a cool color.

Do you avoid a certain combo of colors?

Pick a warm and cool color to focus on contrast.

Remember the old saying, "Never wear blue and brown together"? How can you make them work together?

Scrappy Nova, Shelly Sutton, 2011, 17″ × 17″

Shelly is very good at mixing her warm and cool colors for great contrast. Her quilts tend to have a bright, eye-popping element that I love.

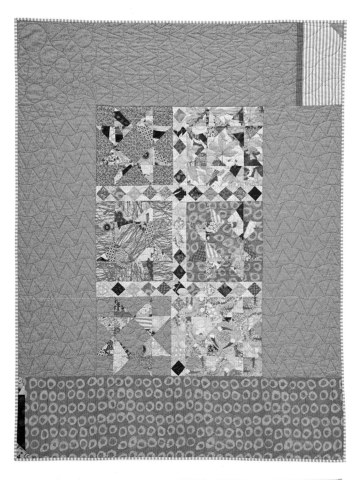

Running with Falling Stars, Victoria Findlay Wolfe, quilted by Linda Sekerak, 2011, 48″ × 62″

I chose a very warm color of gold to mix with different pinks and purples and then added in gray to *pop*! Playing with the purples gave this quilt contrast and a sparkling effect.

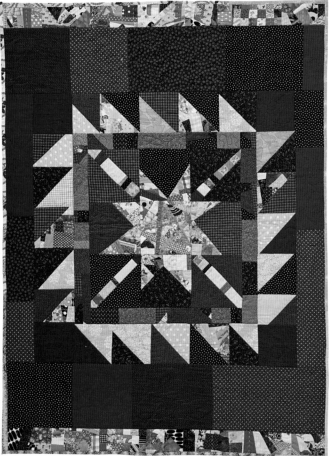

Blue Shining Star, Alexis Coronetz Ortega, 2011, 41″ × 55″

Alexis's big, warm star really dances on the cool blue background.

Fussy Cuts

CHALLENGE #5

Use fussy cutting.

Find a fabric that has great fussy-cut potential. How can you incorporate the fussy-cut fabric into your quilt blocks? How can you expand on the pattern—and not just by cutting around it? Can you add to the design through piecing, quilting, or embellishing? Take it to a level other than just framing your fussy-cut fabrics.

I buy fabric purely because I love it, not because I know what to do with it. Have you ever done that?

Fussy cuts are wonderful for I Spy quilts. You could use the fussy cut as the center and then use the five-sided technique (page 40).

What if you go *big*? Have you tried working with large-scale prints? They can be challenging. If you don't have any, you could do a fabric swap to find something new and different.

15 Minutes to Play and Contemplate

Will the shape or the colors of the fussy cut inspire you?

Will its design influence your quilting?

Why not doodle for inspiration?

Use the patterns in the fussy cut or in an inspiration fabric to guide your quilting.

Can you add your own paper-pieced design to add to the fussy-cut image?

Have you tried appliqué or collage?

For Victoria, with Buttons, LeeAnn Decker, 2011, 24″ × 24″

LeeAnn and I did a fussy-cut swap challenge. I sent her this big red poppy to inspire her. LeeAnn made red fabric blocks and then incorporated the slashing technique (page 58) with various tones of red. She took advantage of the white polka dots to include button embellishments. Then she hand quilted the piece to reflect her slashing lines. She also added fuzzy French knots to the center of the poppy for dimension.

Made for LeeAnn, Victoria Findlay Wolfe, 2011, 24″ × 24″

LeeAnn sent me a vintage piece of floral fabric with cut-off scrolls. I appliquéd extensions of the scrolls and included embroidery to expand on the idea. I also used free-motion quilting to add yet another element of scrolls and flowers.

Bumps in the Night, Victoria Findlay Wolfe, quilted by Linda Sekerak, 2010, 61″ × 61″

Fussy cutting the ghoulish figures made for a fun way to accent holiday-themed fabric using the five-sided technique (page 40). Push it further by taking the Made-Fabric concept all the way through the entire design of the quilt.

Mary in the Garden, Victoria Findlay Wolfe,
2011, 29½˝ × 33½˝

This quilt incorporates many of the techniques described in this book. It was inspired by the Mary fabric panel. Next, Jackie Kunkel gave me the circular-pieced aura around Mary, which led to me insetting radiating red points and fussy-cut flowers into the blue free-pieced sky. I asked friends to send me roses, which I appliquéd over the top. For the grotto, free-pieced fabrics dot the bottom that Mary rests on. Mary is also a reference to my grandmother Elda, who had a Bathtub Mary in her garden.

Mary in the Bathtub, photo by Victoria Findlay Wolfe

What? You've never heard of a Bathtub Mary?

People take their old bathtubs and plant them on-end in their garden, so they can set a statue of Mary inside it, like a shrine. Grandma Elda always had a sense of humor about keeping Mary freshly painted every summer in her garden bathtub.

Why Did I Buy That?

> ## CHALLENGE #6
>
> *Use fabric you don't think you can use.*

Beauty is in the eye of the scissors. Chop it up!

Most quilters have fabric that isn't their favorite and they don't think they can use. Why is using these fabrics a good challenge? Generally, it is because doing so will force you to try ideas that make you really think about your work. You are forced to work with colors you don't like and to find ways to make patterns that you no longer like … great.

You just imagine you won't like the quilt if you use the fabric. But when you slice it up and add new colors and new fabrics, what happens will surprise you. That fabric may become the star of the show, and you might wish you had more (maybe)!

15 Minutes to Play and Contemplate

What don't you like about the fabric?

If the colors were in a different print, would you like it?

Can you combine it with other fabrics to boost the colors that you *do* like?

Focus on how to give that challenge fabric a new reason to be a glorious fabric!

Will you chop it up, throw it into a pile, and sew it all back together to make scrappy Made-Fabric blocks?

I dug through my stash to find some old fabrics that I thought I'd never use. I was surprised at how nice they looked when I cut them up.

Trumpet of the Swan, Victoria Findlay Wolfe, quilted by Shelly Pagliai, 2011, 68″ × 68″

I challenged myself: Not only did I use fabrics that I didn't care for by themselves, but I also mitered the corners of the dark and light pink strip border perfectly and matched up the yellow-and-white print border fabric into sections so the print looks seamless.

Never Say Never

Make the quilt you said you'd never make.

At some point, you will make that quilt anyway!

This has been something that has happened to me over and over. Whenever I say I will never make a …, I end up making three!

Once you get over your fear of making mistakes, your creativity will go wild.

I had a list going in my head of things I thought I'd never make:

A cow quilt

A purple and gold quilt

An entirely paper-pieced quilt

Done, done, and done.

I have loved the experience every time I have done a "never would I make" quilt.

My eleven-year-old daughter said she would *never* be a quilter, but that has not stopped her from making her fourth quilt.

15 Minutes to Play and Contemplate

What are three things you said you'd never make?

Why have you said you wouldn't make them?

Is it a technique you thought you'd never do?

What technique can you learn if you *do* make it?

What's really stopping you?

Go for it!

Skip, Sue, Skip! Margaret Cibulsky, 2011, 12½″ × 12½″

I asked Margaret one day, "What is the one thing you said you'd never make?" She very quickly said, "A Sunbonnet Sue!"

Cupcake Master Pieced, Beatrice Findlay, quilted by Victoria Findlay Wolfe, 2011, 14″ × 19″

I Will Not Make a Cow Quilt, Victoria Findlay Wolfe, 2011, 25″ × 22″

As I was looking at a quilt full of appliqué animals, I said to my friend, "I can guarantee you that I will never make a cow quilt. Why would I do that?" Then I learned just how perfect this challenge is. It forced me to think outside my comfort zone to approach exactly how I would make a cow quilt. And, frankly, I had so much fun making this quilt that I may make a few more!

Something Old, Something New!

Mix up your new blocks with your old blocks and find a way to bring the past to the present.

From orphans to antiques—are you wondering what you will ever do with the quilt blocks you have been storing? Are you curious about where and if ever they will live somewhere some day? Why not dig them out and challenge yourself to make them into something new and wonderful?

In *Something Old, Something New* (below), old and new fabrics and blocks work wonderfully together.

15 Minutes to Play and Contemplate

Look for inspiration in quilt books of old quilts.

Do you recognize some styles that are being represented now in an updated way?

How can you incorporate your Made-Fabric into a new, modern version of an old quilt?

How can you put your spin on it to make it unique to you?

Have you tried appliqué?

This would be a great place to play with new fabrics in a traditional way.

Look for fabrics that relate to your quilt's story.

Try large scale! Play with the sizes of your blocks.

Something Old, Something New, Victoria Findlay Wolfe, quilted by Angela Walters, 2011, 87″ × 91″

This quilt was a play on the grandmother's flower garden quilt. I used a variety of fabrics to make a fast, scrappy Made-Fabric background. I cut Made-Fabric pieces using a large hexagon template for the flowers, and I incorporated vintage flower garden blocks into the new flowers and in the center of the quilt. I joined the giant hexagons and then needle-turn appliquéd them down. One fabric print that helped inspire this was a hexagon bee honeycomb fabric, which I incorporated into the design.

Sunny Delight, Victoria Findlay Wolfe, 2009, 47˝ × 32˝

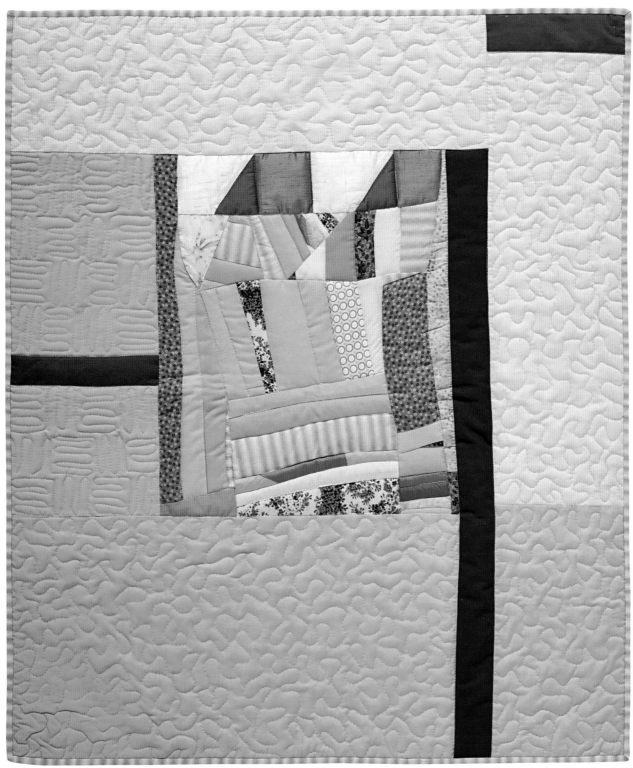

Sherbet, Victoria Findlay Wolfe, 2010, 30″ × 35″

When I made *Sunny Delight* (page 82), I had a lot of leftover, cut-off bits that I saved. A year later, I took those scraps and gave them a new look (in the above quilt)—making something from my *old* scraps into something *new*.

Summer of Stars, Victoria Findlay Wolfe, quilted by Linda Sekerak, 2011, 102″ × 98″

I used a diamond as my starter shape to make Fast-and-Easy Made-Fabric (page 44), then I used a template to cut the large diamonds for the star. I also incorporated Made-Fabric with vintage cross blocks to go around the radiating center. Can you spot the Made-Fabric in the border?

Movement

This challenge should inspire you to focus on the movement in your quilt. Make the quilt dance! Often, movement happens naturally in a scrap quilt. But this challenge offers you a chance to focus on the specific directions in which things move across your quilt. Try incorporating more than one technique. Have you tried embroidery on your quilt blocks to add movement? Have you drawn your own undulating paper-pieced geese? Have you looked at shapes on your print fabrics and noticed how the design can create movement based on how it is placed on your quilt?

15 Minutes to Play and Contemplate

Color play—where is it placed, and how much of it is used in your quilt?

Can you calm something that is very busy by adding a brightest or darkest value?

Does your original block radiate? How can you add to that by your choices of color?

Try gradating your color palette.

Try stripes or slashing. Pay close attention to how you lay out your pieces when you make fabric—do you slant them or overlap them? Try adding something that breaks a border to move your eye from one side of the quilt to the other.

Inspired Spokes, Victoria Findlay Wolfe, 2011, 12˝ × 12˝

Crazy Dresden, Brenda Suderman, 2011, 12˝ × 12˝

Homeward Bound, Chris Hudson, 2011, 12˝ × 12˝

Coming and Going, Victoria Findlay Wolfe, quilted by Linda Sekerak, 2011, 51˝ × 63˝

I started this quilt intending for it to be entirely Flying Geese. At the same time, I had made a mini quilt for another challenge. I had them on the wall next to each other…. And, well, the rest is history!

Medallion Quilts

Have you ever made a small quilt and stopped working on it because it just felt like it needed to be bigger, but you didn't know what it needed next? Have you ever made some blocks and then decided the color palette was wrong, so you cast them aside? How about pulling them back out to make a medallion quilt?

Sometimes I put pieces away for a while and come back to them later. Don't get down about being stuck. Just put it away and wait for a new day—and new eyes—to spark inspiration for your next work of art.

15 Minutes to Play and Contemplate

What orphan blocks do you have that you can make into a medallion?

Can you mix old blocks with new blocks to make a medallion?

Can you combine elements from two or three other quilts to make one?

Have you started a quilt and lost interest? How can that quilt be the start of something new and fabulous?

Can old blocks or an abandoned project become a perfect border?

True North, Victoria Findlay Wolfe with 15 Minute Scrap Bee block contributors: LeeAnn Decker, Glenda Parks, Sujata Shaw, Margaret Cibulsky, Shelly Pagliai, Charlotte Pountney, Mary Ramsey Keasler, Helen Beall, Brenda Suderman, Lynn O'Brien, and Beth Shibley; quilted by Shannon Baker, 2010, 73″ × 75″

This quilt started as two different quilts. All of the blocks sat on my design wall, side by side, for weeks. After leaving them for a while and just looking at them every now and then, I began to realize that it should be *one* quilt—and a new series of play began. I asked myself: What if I incorporated the blocks into the quilt? What If I made the stars into a medallion? What if I set them on point? What if I added the slashed pieced blocks around the border? And so on, until the quilt fell into place.

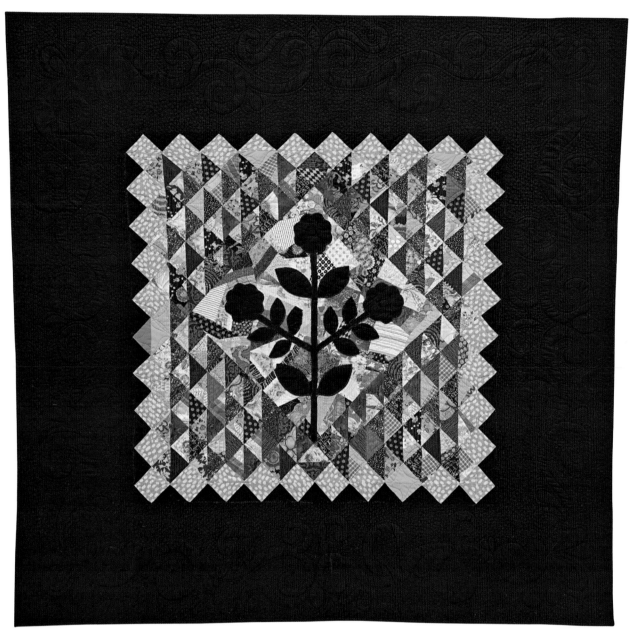

Black Flowers in the Sky, Victoria Findlay Wolfe, quilted by Angela Walters, 2011, 65″ × 65″

At a sewing retreat, I started piecing Made-Fabric from pinks that I was finding in the group's combined scrap pile. (It's always fun to dig through other's scraps for inspiration!) Many of the pinks had gold or yellow tones with them—two colors I wouldn't normally put together. After I made one large piece of fabric, I decided it was so pretty, I couldn't cut it up. So it became the center medallion. I added black to set it off, knowing I wanted to end with big black borders for some great detailed quilting. The medallion needed a punch of *wow* in the middle to match the boldness of the black borders, so I added some black silhouette flowers with black embroidery on the edge of the flowers to add the last bit of *zing* that it needed.

Intuition Quilts

> ### CHALLENGE #11
> *Build a quilt purely on intuition.*

in·tu·i·tion (noun)

To look inside and contemplate. To trust you have the answer without reason but by knowing.

By this far in the book, you should be more aware of yourself as a quilter and trust that you have the creative energy needed to make quilts that are uniquely you. Making anything means you are an artist—claim that title!

Find an inspiration piece of fabric. Have you ever picked up a piece of fabric and thought, "This needs to be a whole quilt"?

Find one thing that inspires you—something small.

Ask yourself, "What is it that inspires me about it?"

Is it "that feeling"? Do you just *know* that it excites you?

Don't think about it. Don't make planned decisions. Just pick up fabric, and when it feels right, sew it together. Just go with it.

Intuition Quilt, Victoria Findlay Wolfe, quilted by Linda Sekerak, 2011, 93˝ × 94˝

Three squares of plaid was all it took to set this quilt in motion.

Listening to your instinct is a process that can be learned, practiced, and enjoyed. Really!

It will feel uncomfortable and uneasy, and it will get you to break a few rules. That's okay. Trust your eyes, not just your head.

Be gentle with yourself.

Know that it's just a quilt, and you can make more.

Make mistakes!

Be selfish with your creativity. Play!

Break the rules.

Be open to your feelings, but take the first step.

Find a new layout by thinking about arrangements you have not used before.

What can you do to come up with a new layout?

Your intuition is talking to you. Are you listening?

Do you act on it? Or do you move on to something else more planned out because that is what you've learned?

How do you capture that moment of following your intuition and let it lead you?

Make a quilt without a pattern? What? Really?

Yes, you can do it!

I hope you are inspired to try something new. Have you already scoured your fabric stash and pulled out fabrics that have ignited an idea? Go with what *feels* right. You have the answers within. Trust that you can make those decisions.

Hooked on a Feeling, Shelly Pagliai, 2011, 66″ × 66″

Shelly started with a piece of Made-Fabric and then incorporated circles she had found in her scrap bin. She felt it was too dull, so she tried a few reds before settling on the bright one. Her inspiration stalled briefly until she began asking herself more "what if" questions and following her gut feeling—her inspiration was ignited once again.

Self Portrait, Miki Willa, 2011, 48″ × 50″

Miki laid out her various orphan and Made-Fabric blocks as she started putting this quilt together. She then added purples from a different project she was working on and found that they worked nicely together. She then focused on adding a few light pieces to keep the sparkle dancing around the quilt.

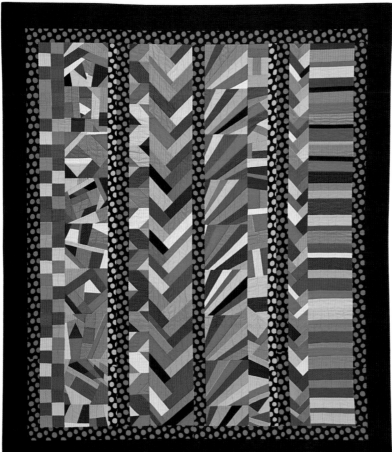

Carnival, Karen Griska, 2006, 49″ × 56″

Using many styles of Made-Fabric sections, Karen followed her intuition to make an exciting quilt that dances to its own beat.

Bea's Knees in the Garden, Victoria Findlay Wolfe, quilted by Angela Walters, 2011, 56″ × 56″

I had made the center square while playing with appliqué for my daughter, but I couldn't decide how to move forward on it. I put it away for a year and then revisited it with new eyes—and my daughter's eyes. She liked what I had done with my *Intuition Quilt* (page 89), and I decided to follow the same format in that quilt for this one. Follow your intuition!

In Closing

I have shared ways to look at your creative process in a new light. I encourage you to throw caution to the wind and try new ideas, crazy color combinations, and as many techniques as you dare. The more freedom you give yourself with the "rules" of quilting, the more you may find that your quilts are truly and uniquely you.

Any time you start a new project, always think about what else you can do to make a quilt different and exciting. What questions can you ask yourself? What are you trying and not trying? What *fun* can you have and how can you learn today through 15 minutes of trying a new technique?

You have a creative voice—let it ring out loud and clear.

Find a way each day to take 15 minutes to stay connected to your process, so that when you do have more time to play, you will be in the mind space of creativity.

You can do it! Go for it!

And remember …

A person who never made a mistake, never tried anything new.

—*Albert Einstein*

Crown of Thorns, Victoria Findlay Wolfe, quilted by Linda Sekerak, 2011, 71″ × 71″

The beginning of this quilt was an unfinished challenge. It sat in my orphan box as a nine-block panel, waiting for the day inspiration would strike. Sometimes quilts, or our eyes, need to mature on their own for a year or two before we know just what to do to them. A year after I made the nine-block center panel, I pulled it out and knew exactly what I needed to do with the large pile of stripes I had already gathered. The stripes made an exciting border around the six-sided shape that related to the center of the crowns. And that last bit of play finished off one of my now-favorite quilts.

About the Author

Victoria Findlay Wolfe, painter, photographer, and quilter, was raised on a farm in rural Minnesota. She learned to sew and quilt when she was four years old. Her grandmother and mother were quilters, and her father, a farmer, also had an upholstery business. Victoria graduated from the College of Visual Arts with a bachelor's degree in Fine  Arts in St. Paul, Minnesota, in 1993. A year later, she arrived in New York City.

After some success as a painter, she discovered quilting blogs, returned to quilting, and started receiving commissions. Seeking the company of other quilters, she founded her blog, bumblebeansinc.blogspot.com. To satisfy a response to her creative philosophy, she started her teaching site, www.15minutesplay.com.

Victoria began an outreach program for a housing project in the South Bronx, New York, through which hundreds of quilts have been made and donated from quilters worldwide (see www.bumblebeansbasics.com). In addition, 60 quilts were auctioned to raise more than $30,000 for the Acacia Network (formerly BASICS/Promesa).*

Victoria is currently the president of the New York Metro Mod Quilt Guild and a member of New York City Empire Quilters and Minnesota Quilt Guild. She is also on the board of directors for the Alliance of American Quilts. Victoria lives in Manhattan with her husband, Michael Findlay, an art dealer, and their daughter, Beatrice.

*Acacia Network (formerly BASICS/Promesa) is a community development corporation whose mission is to enable residents in urban settings, utilizing their programs and services, to become self-sufficient citizens who contribute to the quality of life of their communities.

Books That Inspire Me

The following books are wonderful inspiration. Many are now out of print, but they can be found used or may be available in your local library.

Adamson, Jeremy, *Calico & Chintz, Antique Quilts from the Collection of Patricia S. Smith.* Smithsonian Institution, National Museum of American Art, 1998.

Aller, Allie, *Allie Aller's Crazy Quilting.* C&T Publishing, 2011.

Atkins, Jacqueline M., and Phyllis A. Tepper, *New York Beauties: Quilts from the Empire State.* Dutton Studio, 1992.

Beardsley, John, William Arnett, Paul Arnett, and Jane Lliingston, *The Quilts of Gee's Bend.* Tinwood Books, 2002.

Huws, Edrica, *Edrica Huws Patchworks.* Manaman, 2007.

Laury, Jean Ray, *Quilts and Coverlets: A Contemporary Approach.* Van Nostrand Reinhold, 1971.

Leon, Eli, *Accidentally on Purpose: The Aesthetic Management of Irregularities in African Textiles and African-American Quilts.* Figge Art Museum, 2007.

Marston, Gwen, *Liberated Quiltmaking.* American Quilter's Society, 1996.

Montano, Judith Baker, *The Crazy Quilt Handbook, Revised 2nd Edition.* C&T Publishing, 2001.

Roy, Gerald E., *Quilts by Paul D. Pilgrim: Blending the Old & the New.* American Quilter's Society, 1997.

Wahlman, Maude Southwell, *Signs & Symbols: African Images in African American Quilts, 2nd Edition.* Tinwood Books, 2001.

Waldvogel, Merikay, and Barbara Brackman, *Patchwork Souvenirs of the 1933 World's Fair.* Thomas Nelson, 1993.

Great Titles *from* C&T PUBLISHING & stashBOOKS.

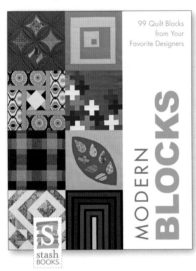

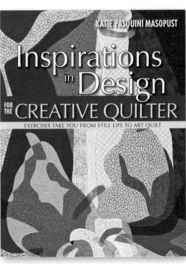

Available at your local retailer or **www.ctpub.com** *or* **800-284-1114**